ANIMAL KINGDOM

Nicholas Blechman

Researched by
Simon Rogers

B P P

ANIMAL
KINGDOM

180°

Nicholas
Blechman

INTRODUCTION

From the great blue whale to the tiniest insect (and of course, to humankind), we are all connected by the tree of life, having evolved over millions of years from tiny basic organisms that lived on Earth more than 3.4 billion years ago.

Millions of animal species have been identified, but scientists are still making thousands of new discoveries each year. With many of these new species hidden in the depths of rain forests that are now under threat from humankind, some may become extinct before we even knew they existed.

Every single one of these animals has found its own unique place in nature and has adapted to survive in its particular environment, developing its shape, color, way of reproducing, diet, and abilities through the incredible process of evolution.

This book introduces you to extraordinary animals from around the world and some of the best facts and figures to be found in nature, brought to life by incredible information graphics. So turn the page to understand the facts in the blink of an eye.

SPECIES

The animal kingdom is made up of an amazing array of different creatures.

Animals are set apart from plants by their ability to move freely, the presence of a central nervous system, and their need to consume other living organisms to survive.

There are two main types of animal: vertebrates, which have a backbone, and invertebrates, which do not. The vertebrate and invertebrate families can be divided into smaller groups, like reptiles, birds, or mammals, that are made up of different species with similar features.

Different species have developed unique traits over billions of years through evolution, meaning that all the hugely varied animals share a common starting point billions of years ago.

While most of this book looks at the amazing characteristics of individual species, here is a look at how animals have developed into different groups and why.

ORIGIN OF SPECIES

Darwin recognized that different animal species had unique adaptations that made them perfectly suited to their particular environment. For instance, birds' beaks are shaped differently depending on what they eat.

Charles Darwin studied animals to learn more about evolution. He spent his life looking at the differences between the amazing variety of species on Earth.

Eats seeds

Eats insects

Eats fruit

WIN THE DAY

In nature, every species wants to pass on its genes and produce offspring. However, in the wild, many animals die before they reach full maturity—the time when they can mate and reproduce. With so many animals on Earth, there is a lot of competition to survive.

NATURAL SELECTION

Being able to endure tougher conditions, being faster at finding food, or being better at hiding from predators could all improve an animal's chances of surviving into maturity. These superior characteristics will also catch the eye of a mate, who will want to pass those strengths on to its young. This process is known as natural selection.

ONE AND ONLY

Darwin realized that over thousands of years, animals' characteristics had become refined, making each species uniquely adapted to its environment.

This book is packed with examples of animals that have developed some amazing features.

FAST AND FURIOUS

Speed and strength are useful for catching dinner.

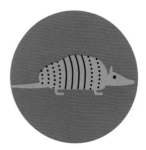

SELF DEFENSE

Having good armor makes an animal less likely to become somebody else's meal.

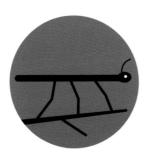

UNDER COVER

A well-camouflaged animal is less likely to be spotted by a predator.

LEG UP

A physical advantage that provides greater access to food reduces the risk of starvation.

SHOW OFF

Being more attractive to a mate increases an animal's chances of passing on its genes.

STRETCH YOUR LEGS

Humans have their own evolution story, developing from early primates into the walking, talking, deep-thinking species that we are today.

CLASS OF THEIR OWN

WARM-BLOODED ANIMALS
regulate the temperature
of their bodies.

· ·

The animal kingdom comprises
millions of different species
of animals. These species can
be sorted into different groups,
each of which has developed a
similar set of characteristics.

IN FINE FEATHER
Birds are warm-blooded
vertebrates.

They breathe
with lungs.

They have beaks.

They have a
pair of wings.

They reproduce by
laying fertilized eggs,
which primarily hatch
in nests.

They have
two feet.

They have
feathers, which
help them to fly
and/or swim.

FUR COAT

Mammals are warm-blooded vertebrates.

Most have fur or hair.

They are suited to living either on land or in the water.

The females give birth to live young and produce milk to nourish them.

They breathe with their lungs — meaning that dolphins and other mammals that live in the water need to hold their breath and come up for air.

Most have four limbs.

Most have a tail.

HAVE SOME BACKBONE

Vertebrates have backbones and a complex brain, making them the most advanced organisms on the planet.

Although vertebrates only make up 3 percent of the animal kingdom, there are around 62,000 different vertebrate species, each one perfectly adapted to its environment. The most intelligent vertebrate of all is you — a human being!

BLOOD RUNNING COLD

Cold-blooded animals take on the temperature of their surroundings. Many need to bask in the sun in order to keep their body temperature up.

TWIN FINS
Fish are vertebrates, suited to living underwater. Most are cold-blooded.

Fins and a tail help fish to swim through the water.

They breathe with gills.

They reproduce by laying eggs.

Most are covered in waterproof scales.

FROG PRINCE

Amphibians are cold-blooded vertebrates.

They can live in water or on land.

Amphibians have small lungs, but mostly breathe through their skin.

Most have four limbs. Some have none.

Some reproduce by laying eggs. Some give birth to live young.

OFF THE SCALE

Reptiles are cold-blooded vertebrates.

They are suited to living either on land or in the water.

They breathe with lungs.

They have varying number of limbs — some, such as snakes, have none at all!

Almost all reproduce by laying eggs.

They are covered in hard scales.

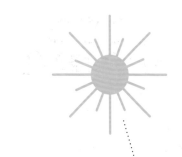

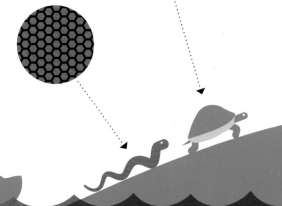

TOTALLY SPINELESS
· · · · · · · · · · · · · · · · · · · ·

Invertebrates have no backbone, although most of them can move. Some—like coral—look like plants, but they have no cell walls and cannot make their own food for energy, so are classified as animals.

NINE LIVES

There are nine main categories of invertebrate, which together make up 97 percent of all the species on Earth.

SPONGE BATH

Although they don't have organs, such as lungs or a heart, **porifera** are still classed as animals. They live in the water and feed on small organisms.

SHELL SUIT

Mollusks, such as clams and snails, are suited to living either on land or in the water. Most have shells, soft bodies, and no legs.

NASTY STING

Cnidarians, such as jellyfish, live in the water and are armed with stinging cells to ward off predators.

FLAT PACK

Platyhelminths are flatworms with soft, segmented bodies. Half of these species are parasitic, stealing nutrients from their host animals and causing disease.

ROUND THE TWIST

Nematodes are tiny roundworms. Some, such as hookworm or *Loa loa*, can cause disease in humans.

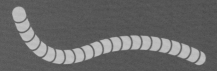

SUPER STAR

Echinoderms have thousands of tiny feet on their arms, and can regrow a severed limb. They live in salt water.

NO LEG TO STAND ON

Annelids are segmented worms with no legs, and can be found in water or on land.

SINGLE CELL

Because they feed on other organisms and can move around, **protozoa** are considered animal-like. They consist of just one cell and have no limbs or other features.

POD SQUAD

Three-quarters of the creatures in the world are **arthropods!** Crabs, spiders, and insects are all arthropods, with segmented bodies and six or more legs.

SENSES

Animals use their senses to make smart choices, so they can find food without wasting too much energy, find a mate, and stay safe when it matters most.

Avoiding your predators or finding your prey isn't just about strength and speed—often it's about knowing they are coming or outwitting them by using your superior senses.

Some animals have senses that are similar to those of humans, but much more precise. Others have adapted to explore the world using senses that seem strange and different from our own, such as echolocation, night-vision, and ultrasound, which are useful for finding your way in the dark or living underwater.

Sometimes an animal's reliance on a particular sense has led to the species developing a particular feature. In this chapter, find out who has a star-shaped nose and which animal has eyes the size of dinner plates!

SEEING

Some animals rely on a strong sense of sight to survive, whether to spot prey or notice a predator coming. But different needs and different habitats have caused animals' eyesight to develop in different ways.

GOT IT COVERED

Dragonflies have huge eyes that almost cover their whole head. These are made up of 30,000 optical units called ommatidia. They can see colors that humans can't, such as ultraviolet (UV) light.

ALL-SEEING

Chameleons have eyes that they can move and focus independently, which gives them nearly 360-degree vision.

BLIND SPOT

Rhinoceroses have terrible eyesight and cannot see a person standing still if they are more than 100 feet/ 30 meters away. As their eyes are on opposite sides of their head, they have to look with one eye at a time to see straight ahead.

UNDER ITS SKIN

Mole rats live underground and rely on their other senses. Their small eyes are covered entirely by skin, which makes them truly blind.

WIDE-EYED

Tarsiers have the largest eye-to-body ratio of any mammal. This makes their head heavy, so they wait silently to catch their prey.

Their eyes are fixed in their skulls and can't turn in their sockets. Instead, tarsiers use their flexible neck to rotate their head 180 degrees.

OPEN WIDE

With wide-set eyes, an **eagle's** field of vision is much wider than a human's . . .

allowing the eagle to clearly see an object at 20 feet/6 meters that a human could only see with the same precision at 5 feet/1.5 meters away.

LOOK FORWARD

Forward-facing eyes and stereoscopic vision allows **tawny owls** to determine depth and solidity.

BIRD'S-EYE VIEW

Eagles can spot prey from 2 miles/3.2 kilometers away.

GOOD LOOKING

Hammerhead sharks have unbeatable all-around vision. The location of their eyes gives them a 360-degree look at the world.

360°

BROUGHT TO LIGHT

Colossal squid live about 3,200 feet/975 meters under the sea, where sunlight doesn't reach. They have the biggest eyes in the animal world— 11.8 inches/30 centimeters across— which let them see in the darkness of the deep ocean. They also have light organs called photophores that act like headlights.

Tawny owls have the best developed eyes of all vertebrates. Their vision is one hundred times more sensitive at low light levels than a human's.

As they dive to catch prey, their eye muscles continuously refocus the eyeball to keep a razor-sharp lock on their victims.

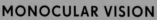

MONOCULAR VISION

Most animals of prey have monocular vision, with eyes on either side of their head. This lets them see two scenes at the same time, to stay alert to predators. While they can still see an object in the distance, they cannot tell exactly how far away the object is.

BINOCULAR VISION

Most carnivorous mammals and all birds of prey have binocular vision, with two eyes that both face forward. Binocular vision allows predators to hone in on prey, quickly and accurately determining striking distance.

HEARING

Animals have developed their hearing
to be able to do some amazing things.
They use their heightened sense of
hearing to hunt, communicate, and find
their way around.

NIGHT OWL

Tawny owls hunt
at night in total
darkness.

This is thanks to
large earholes located
at slightly different
levels, giving them
directional hearing,
which lets them work
out exactly where a
sound is coming from.

Their hearing
is ten times better
than a human's.

NO LOVE LOST

Elephants have great
hearing, which they
need in order to
communicate across
distances more than
1 mile/1.6 kilometers.

This is important when
a female wants to let
males know that she is
ready to mate, which
only happens every four
to five years.

They use infrasonic
sounds, which are
too deep for a human
ear to hear.

HUNT HIGH AND LOW

Cats have thirty-two
muscles in their ears,
giving them the ability
to rotate each one 180
degrees in separate
directions. This allows
them to pick up sounds
and work
out where they are
coming from.

A cat can detect
higher-pitched sounds
than humans can,
making them able to
hear the noises small
rodents might make.

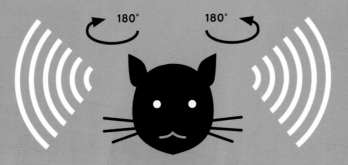

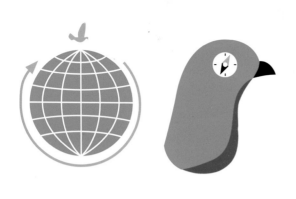

HOME STRAIGHT

Homing pigeons can fly back thousands of miles to reach home from places they have never even been before.

Scientists think that particles of iron in a pigeon's beak act like a compass, aligning north with the earth's magnetic field and helping the bird to navigate home.

In the past, this ability made pigeons useful in carrying messages over long distances quickly, as a pigeon would fly home with a thin scroll of paper attached to its leg.

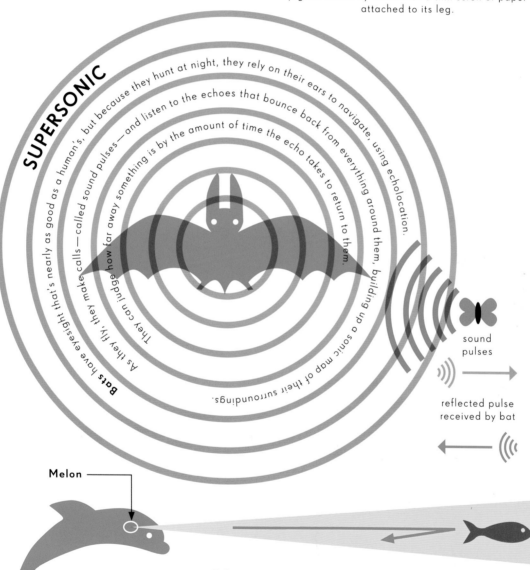

SUPERSONIC

Bats have eyesight that's nearly as good as a human's, but because they hunt at night, they rely on their ears to navigate, using echolocation. As they fly, they make calls—called sound pulses—and listen to the echoes that bounce back from everything around them, building up a sonic map of their surroundings. They can judge how far away something is by the amount of time the echo takes to return to them.

sound pulses

reflected pulse received by bat

Melon

SOUNDING OUT

A **dolphin** hunts using a similar technique to that of bats, letting out high-pitched clicks from an organ inside its head called a melon. The dolphin listens for an echo returning from any object in its path to pinpoint the object's whereabouts.

23

BEING NOSEY

A good sense of smell is useful for all sorts of things: finding food, sensing danger, or seeking a mate.

REMARKABLE SHARKS
Sharks can smell chemicals that fish give out to warn one another of danger and can detect blood from more than 1 mile/1.6 kilometers away.

ON THE SCENT
The surface area dedicated to sensing smell is seventy-six times bigger in a **bloodhound** than it is in a human, with four billion olfactory nerves (for smelling), compared to the twelve million a human has.

LED BY THE NOSE
The **silvertip grizzly bear** has a sense of smell seven times better than a bloodhound! It can smell prey up to 18 miles/29 kilometers away, and can detect its presence for up to forty-eight hours after the animal has left the scene.

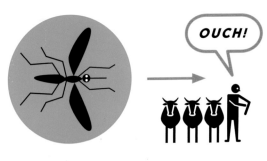

OUCH!

IN THE BULL PEN
Mosquitoes have a sense of smell 10,000 times better than a human's. When we exhale, we let out carbon dioxide and lactic acid that mosquitoes can detect, allowing them to search out a human in a field full of cows.

LOVE IN THE AIR
To attract a mate, female **moths** let out a chemical scent. Male moths can smell this up to 30 miles/48 kilometers away with their antennae, 70 percent of which are dedicated to detecting this scent alone.

TOUCHY SUBJECT

Animals have developed a sense of touch to be able to do things that humans cannot, helping them to survive in the wild.

LUCKY STARS

A **star-nosed mole** has lots of tentacles on its nose, which contain more than 25,000 receptive organs in a space smaller than 0.16 square inch/1 square centimeter. These tentacles are extremely sensitive to touch and electrical impulses, allowing them to find prey without needing a sense of sight.

GOOD VIBRATIONS

Crocodiles have thousands of tiny receptors around their jaws that let them sense the vibrations of prey in the water, helping them to detect and locate their prey.

BY A WHISKER

Catfish have an enhanced sense of touch. Instead of scales, they have smooth skin covered with fine hairs through which they feel.

SEALED FATE

Seals use their whiskers to seek out fish and track them up to 591 feet/180 meters away. They have more nerve fibers in their whiskers than any other whiskered creature.

RECORD BREAKERS

The world is full of creatures that have evolved in extraordinary ways and developed enhanced abilities to ensure their own survival. Whether it's due to their strength, speed, or sheer size, each sector of the animal kingdom has its own set of record breakers.

To avoid becoming somebody else's meal, some animals seek safety in numbers and swarm together in tightly packed clusters to confuse their predators. Others have learned to defend themselves by launching something off-putting at their attackers.

Hunters, such as the cheetah, sprint at incredible speeds to capture their prey. Grazers, on the other hand, can travel thousands of miles around the globe just to find the best feeding grounds or to raise their young.

Extraordinary, diverse, and sometimes strange, the world is packed with animals that achieve the unimaginable every day. Here is a rundown of some of the animal kingdom's most amazing record breakers.

GROUND HERO

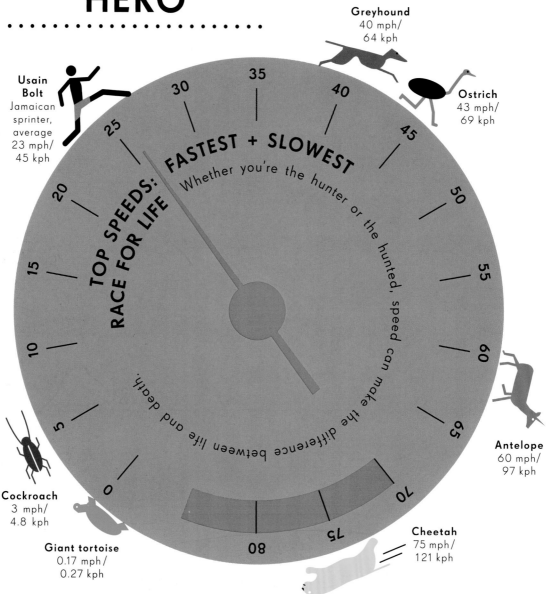

Greyhound
40 mph/
64 kph

Ostrich
43 mph/
69 kph

Usain Bolt
Jamaican sprinter, average 23 mph/ 45 kph

TOP SPEEDS: RACE FOR LIFE

FASTEST + SLOWEST

Whether you're the hunter or the hunted, speed can make the difference between life and death.

35
30
40
25
45
20
50
15
55
10
60
5
65
0
70
08
75

Antelope
60 mph/
97 kph

Cheetah
75 mph/
121 kph

Cockroach
3 mph/
4.8 kph

Giant tortoise
0.17 mph/
0.27 kph

CHAMPION THROWERS

Termites can fire a sticky fluid from their head.

Pistol shrimps can emit powerful streams of bubbles.

Camels can projectile vomit toward a threat.

WEIGHT LIFTERS

Being strong is all relative. Elephants are renowned for their strength, but they are by no means the most impressive weightlifters. Which of these animals can lift the most in comparison to their own body weight?

Rhinoceros Beetle:
85,000 percent

Leaf-cutter ant:
5,000 percent

Bald eagle:
400 percent

Tiger:
200 percent

Elephant:
160 percent

SUPER SWIMMERS
. . . .

SAVE YOUR BREATH
Some animals that live in the water don't have gills, so they have to hold their breath as they swim. Who can last the longest underwater?

Harbor seal
5 minutes

Dolphin
8 minutes

Walrus
10 minutes

Human
22 minutes*

Northern elephant seal
30 minutes

Alligator
2 hours

PACKED LIKE SARDINES
The **sardine** run is one of the biggest coordinated shoaling movements of fish. They spawn near the African coast. The shoals can be up to 4.5 miles/ 7 kilometers long, 1 mile/1.6 kilometers wide, and are visible from space.

When threatened, sardines (and other foraging fish) group together to create huge bait balls of up to 65 feet/20 meters in diameter to confuse their predators.

At 41 feet/12 meters, the **whale shark** is the longest fish in the world.

THE SQUID AND THE WHALE SHARK
A **giant squid** reaches up to 59 feet/18 meters long.

* This is the longest breath-holding time ever recorded for a human being. The average time a human can hold their breath is only around one minute.

Thousands of dolphins feed on the sardine run by herding groups of the fish together like sheepdogs.

The shoaling fish respond to the position of their neighbors, trying not to get too close to some and keeping far enough away from others.

31

TOP FLIGHT

FAST AND FURIOUS

Peregrine falcons have a top speed of 242 mph/389 kph, making them the fastest living thing on Earth.

SAFETY IN NUMBERS

Many birds flock to defend themselves against predators.

1,000,000 red-billed queleas

250,000 starlings

400 lapwings

LIGHT AS A FEATHER?

A **pigeon's** feathers weigh more than its bones.

MAKING MOUNTAINS

Fifty **Canada geese** can produce 2.5 tons/2.25 metric tons of excrement in a year.

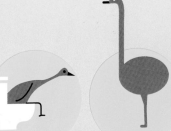

STANDING TALL

The flightless **greater rhea** is the tallest bird in South America at 4 feet/ 1.2 meters.

ON THE FLY

Some species of birds make long journeys each year to find the best conditions for breeding and to avoid harsh winters. Which birds have the most impressive migration routes?

Sooty shearwater   **Arctic tern**   **Pied wheatear**

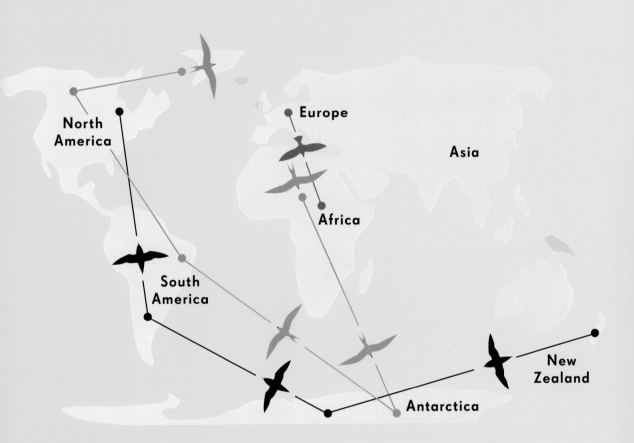

North America

Europe

Asia

Africa

South America

New Zealand

Antarctica

LOST YOUR VOICE?

Only a few species of birds have no voice: storks, pelicans, and some **vultures.**

ON SONG

Birdsong can tell you how healthy a bird is; the more complex the song, the healthier the bird.

BIG THINKERS

The weight of an animal's brain compared to its body can give a basic idea as to that animal's intelligence. How do different animals' brains measure up?

1.5 pounds/ 680 grams

0.4 pounds/ 181 grams

Pig

3.5 pounds/ 1,588 grams

Giraffe

Dolphin

0.3 pounds/ 136 grams

1.3 pounds / 582 grams

Sheep

Hippopotamus

0.07 pounds/ 32 grams

0.004 pounds/ 2 grams

0.0005 pounds/ 0.24 grams

Cat

Rat

Frog

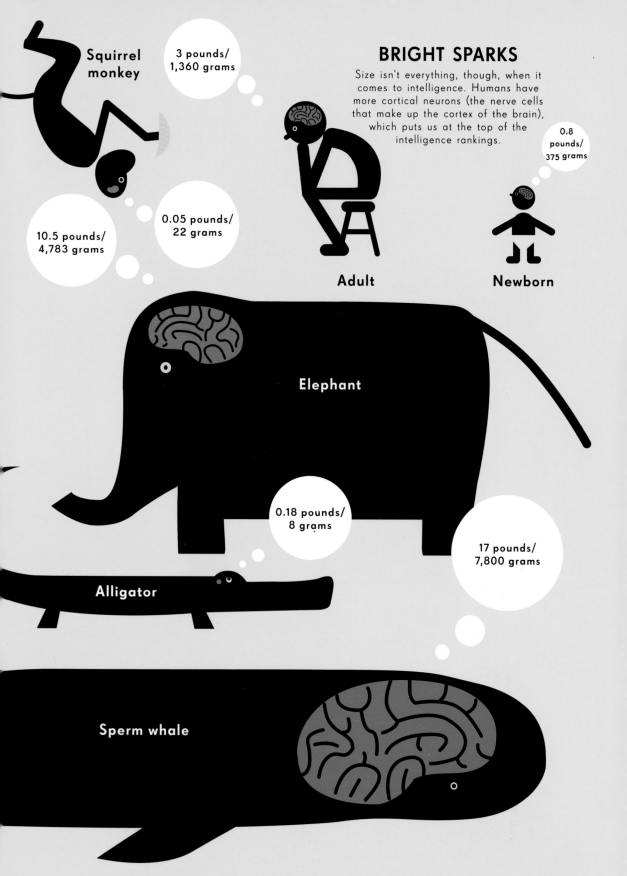

Squirrel monkey

3 pounds/
1,360 grams

BRIGHT SPARKS

Size isn't everything, though, when it comes to intelligence. Humans have more cortical neurons (the nerve cells that make up the cortex of the brain), which puts us at the top of the intelligence rankings.

0.8 pounds/
375 grams

0.05 pounds/
22 grams

10.5 pounds/
4,783 grams

Adult

Newborn

Elephant

0.18 pounds/
8 grams

17 pounds/
7,800 grams

Alligator

Sperm whale

35

FOOD AND DRINK

All animals need food and water to live. But what they consume, how much, and how often can vary wildly.

What an animal eats determines where it fits in the food chain, with predators at the top and their prey beneath them. It also affects the shape and number of their teeth, the length of their tongues, and size of their mouths.

Different animals have different eating patterns. While some, like the kingfisher, eat more than half their body weight in a day, others, like the blue whale, can go for eight months without eating at all!

Here is a look at what some of nature's most interesting beasts have on their menu, and how to tell an herbivore from a carnivore. You never know, it might come in handy one day!

FOOD CHAIN

The food chain is a continuous process. At any moment something is being eaten, dies, breaks down, and is being eaten again. It can never have less than three stages.

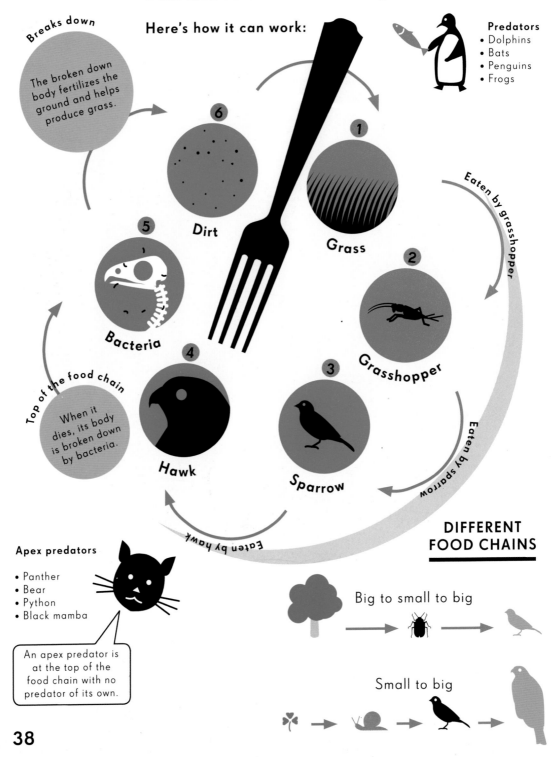

Breaks down

The broken down body fertilizes the ground and helps produce grass.

Here's how it can work:

Predators
- Dolphins
- Bats
- Penguins
- Frogs

6 Dirt

1 Grass

Eaten by grasshopper

5 Bacteria

2 Grasshopper

Top of the food chain

When it dies, its body is broken down by bacteria.

4 Hawk

3 Sparrow

Eaten by sparrow

Eaten by hawk

Apex predators
- Panther
- Bear
- Python
- Black mamba

An apex predator is at the top of the food chain with no predator of its own.

DIFFERENT FOOD CHAINS

Big to small to big

Small to big

38

WHALE-SIZE LUNCH

Blue whales are the largest mammals on Earth. Remarkably, they eat very tiny crustaceans, called krill, almost exclusively. Krill eat phytoplankton, which are microscopic organisms. This means that whales eat much closer to the microscopic level than any other mammal, despite their enormous size.

A blue whale may consume up to 4–8 tons/3.6–7.3 metric tons of food per day during their feeding season.

That's 8,000 pounds/3,629 kilograms of krill per day!

For the other eight months of the year, it apparently doesn't eat anything at all, living off stored fat.

Jan.	Feb.	Mar.	Apr.	May	Jun.	Jul.	Aug.	Sep.	Oct.	Nov.	Dec.

Eats   **Does not eat**

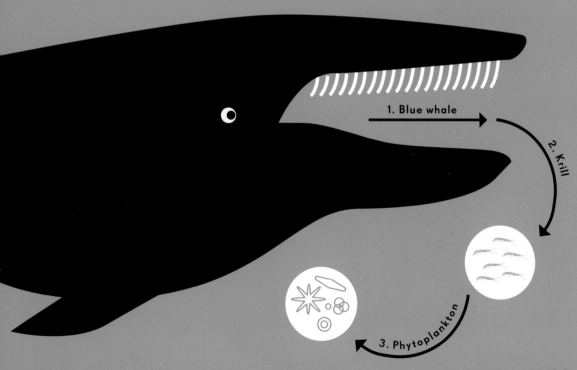

1. Blue whale

2. Krill

3. Phytoplankton

CARNIVORES

Carnivores eat a diet of mainly meat.

Sweat is released through their tongues, as many carnivores hunt at night and therefore don't sweat as much.

Eyes tend to face forward to allow proper depth perception for hunting.

Jaws move up and down but not side to side.

Teeth are sharp, long, and pointed. They are built to tear prey apart.

Saliva contains no digestive enzymes.

Tongue laps up water. Cats can't taste sweet flavors (although dogs can).

FISH FOOD

Piranhas are thought of as carnivorous fish, when in fact they are omnivorous, often eating plants.

Omnivores

Herbivores

Carnivores

HERBIVORES

Herbivores eat a plant-based diet.

Sweat is released through their skin, as herbivore animals tend to gather food during the day.

Eyes are often on the side of the head, to spot danger from behind.

Jaws move up and down and side to side.

Teeth are flat with squared back molars to grind food.

Saliva is alkaline, containing carbohydrate digestive enzymes to predigest and break down plant food.

Tongue can taste sweet things. They suck up water in their mouths.

THINK CARNIVORES ARE THE ONES TO LOOK OUT FOR? THINK AGAIN.

Cape buffalo are short-tempered South African herbivores who will charge attackers such as lions.

Wild boars weigh up to 400 pounds/ 181 kilograms and have sharp tusks.

Hippopotamuses kill more humans than lions, leopards, or crocodiles do.

Male elephants periodically have huge hormone surges that make them violent.

HELP!

OPEN WIDE

BIG MOUTH

A **hippo** can open its mouth to 180 degrees.

TONGUE TWISTER

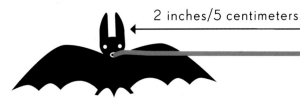

2 inches/5 centimeters

The **tube-lipped nectar bat** has the longest tongue, compared to its body length, of any known mammal.

TONGUE-TIED

The **giraffe** can extend its tongue 18 inches/46 centimeters.

SENSE OF DIRECTION

The **snake's** forked tongue acts as a directional detector that can find other animals in their local environment.

LICKETY SPIT

A **chameleon's** tongue travels at 1,312 feet/400 meters per second squared, about 41 Gs of force. A space shuttle only develops about 3 Gs of force when it takes off.

THREE-TON TONGUE

A **blue whale's** tongue weighs 3 tons/2.7 metric tons.

GRIN AND BEAR IT

How do animals compare when you count the number of teeth they have?

Rat: 16

Rabbit: 28

Human: 32

Crocodile: 70

Burmese python: 100

Dolphin: 252

WHAT A MOUTHFUL

How many types of bacteria are there in the mouths of different animals?

Human mouth

615

Dog mouth

600

Mouse mouth

200

BIG BELLIES

How much do animals eat
compared to the size of their bodies?

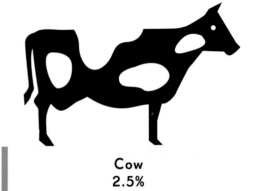

Duck
20%

Walrus
6%

Mouse
15%

Chicken
7.5%

Cow
2.5%

THIRSTY WORK

How much water do
animals consume in a day?

Budgie 0.0085 cups/2 milliliters per day

Turkey 2 cups/470 milliliters per day

Pig 72 cups/17,000 milliliters per day

Polar bear 97 cups/23,000 milliliters per day

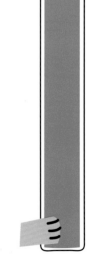

Northern elephant seal 228 cups/54,000 milliliters per day

44

EAT LIKE
A BIRD

A **kingfisher** eats 60 percent
of its body weight in food per day.

A **grizzly bear** eats 12 percent
of its body weight in food per day.

FAMILY

Nothing is more important to a species' survival than its ability to reproduce and the survival of its young. Life can be dangerous for newborns, which has led to many animals developing some creative solutions for looking after their young.

In some cases, the mother and father work together to ensure that their offspring have the best chance of survival—often keeping them safe in nests and feeding them until they're grown and ready to survive on their own.

Other animals, such as wolves, form large extended families. Groups of wolves, called packs, live and hunt together, and all members of the pack benefit from a successful hunt, making teamwork important.

In this section you'll find some family units that are similar to your own, and some that might seem strange. Can you imagine living in a burrow with three hundred of your sisters and brothers? Read on.

BRINGING UP BABY

Animals rear their young in many different ways. Here are some examples:

KICK START

Koalas live alone and the mothers are incredibly protective.

GRR!

Single mom

CHEW IT OVER

Until their babies can process the toxic eucalyptus leaves that the adults eat, a **koala** mom feeds her baby, called a joey, her own droppings to build up its tolerance.

48

Mom   Dad

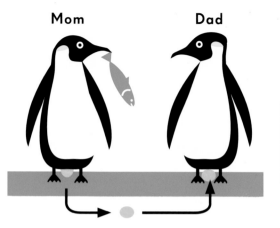

IT TAKES TWO

A female **emperor penguin** lays one egg, which the male incubates by balancing it on his feet under his stomach. The female then searches for food. When the chick is born, mom and dad take turns foraging for food and caring for their young.

POLAR PARTY

Polar bears are solitary, but do gather occasionally in large groups. Baby polar bears live with their mothers for two years after birth.

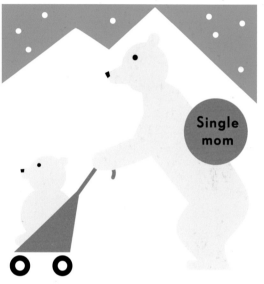

Single mom

Alpha

Beta   Beta

Mates for life

Omega

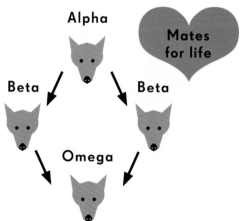

LEADER OF THE PACK

Wolf packs consist of an extended family structure, ruled by male and female alphas who lead the pack.

Just below the alphas in the pack are the beta wolves, who take over if anything happens to the top dogs.

At the bottom of the pack is the omega wolf, who is the last to eat and is bullied by the rest.

CUB CLUB

A **cheetah** mother has two to six cubs per litter. She protectively rears them until they are two years old, then leaves them to fend for themselves and heads off to start a new family elsewhere. Males are less solitary.

Single mom

BABYSITTING

As many as 220 types of bird species and 120 mammals will help to rear others' young, often postponing their own chance to mate. This is called cooperative breeding.

These animals include African wild dogs, chimpanzees, naked mole rats, lions, bee-eaters, kookaburras, pied kingfishers, and Seychelles warblers.

MIND OUT

Meerkat pups grow up in a burrow to be out of danger, with babysitters taking care of them.

When they emerge into the wild, the older meerkats stand around to watch. A sentry stays on duty, looking out for danger.

QUEEN MOTHER

Naked mole rats are the first mammals ever discovered to be eusocial like bees, wasps, and termites. They live in colonies of up to 300. Each group is ruled by a queen, which is the only female able to have babies.

The queen and two to three males reproduce. The rest are workers and are also sterile, meaning that they can't have young themselves. When the queen dies, another female takes her place.

50

NANNY-TASTIC

Starling chicks are often brought up by a single pair of starlings, but sometimes have a helper that serves as a "nanny."

READY IN THE WINGS

Florida scrub jay parents are assisted by up to six non-breeding helpers — usually their offspring from years before.

It works, too! Assisted pairs successfully rear more than one and a half times as many young as those without help.

HEAD OF THE FAMILY

| MATRIARCHAL (led by a female) |
| PATRIARCHAL (led by a male) |

Different animals organize their family units in different ways.

Elephant herd
Size: 6–12

Mouse family
Size: 3–12

MOUSE HOUSE

A female **mouse** looks after her babies for around three weeks after birth before they go their separate ways.

PINK ELEPHANTS

Elephant herds are run by the eldest female, called the matriarch. She leads her daughters and their calves until she dies. Bulls travel together in all-male pods, looking for female families to mate with.

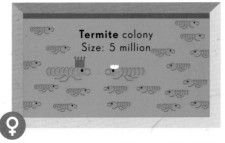

Termite colony
Size: 5 million

TREATED LIKE ROYALTY

Termite colonies are ruled by a queen, who pairs with a king to mate with for life. They are looked after by millions of worker and soldier termites.

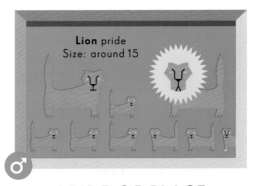

Lion pride
Size: around 15

PRIDE OF PLACE

Lions are the only cats that live in large family groups. They are ruled over by one or two males. The female lionesses do most of the hunting. When male cubs mature, they leave the pride and become nomads, searching out other prides to join.

POD SQUAD

Killer whales have a complex family structure, similar to elephant herds, with pods ruled by females. Offspring often stay with their mothers all their lives. Females can live to age ninety, meaning that as many as four generations can travel together.

Killer whale pod
Size: up to 30

Bonobos family
Size: up to 100

HAPPY FAMILIES

Bonobos are one of the closest relatives to humans and are very social creatures. They live in peaceful, female-led family groups that change all the time as members leave to hunt for food. Different groups may sometimes meet and spend time grooming one another to be friendly.

CURIOSITIES

MIX AND MATCH

Some creatures are able to mate with other species. Their offspring are called hybrids. Here are some examples:

BEEFED UP

Beefalo are hardier than cattle and have a longer life span thanks to their ability to cope with harsher climates and eat a wider variety of foods. They were first found in the wild, but are now bred by humans.

American bison + Cattle = Beefalo

GOOD CAMA

The first **cama** was born in 1998 and was bred by humans to be strong like a camel and woolly like a llama. Unfortunately, camas turned out to be rather irritable.

Camel + Llama = Cama

WILD AND WOOLLY

While some hybrids mix together the characteristics of both its parents, a **geep** has a mosaic of different features, with separate sheep parts that are woolly and goat parts that are hairy.

Goat + Sheep = Geep

RARE WHOLPHIN

There are very few known **wholphins** in the world. Their characteristics fall midway between each parent— right down to their teeth! While a false killer whale has forty-four and a bottlenose dolphin has eighty-eight, a wholphin has sixty-six teeth.

False killer whale + Bottlenose dolphin = Wholphin

BIG FISH

Unlike the huge female **anglerfish** (which has a light-like attachment to attract prey), the male anglerfish is tiny.

TWO BECOME ONE

When the pair mate, the male burrows into the female's body and is eventually absorbed. The unlucky male dies in the process, but his sperm are used to fertilize the female's eggs.

1

2

HABITATS

An animal's habitat is its natural home or environment. Habitats vary wildly around the world, from the hot, humid rain forests to the cold, barren poles.

Climate plays a big role in defining a given habitat; factors such as varying temperatures and annual rainfall determine the types of plants and animals that can live in an area.

Every habitat presents some difficult conditions, whether it be extreme temperatures or limited amounts of food, water, or land. So each species that lives there has adapted to be uniquely in tune with its surroundings.

Humans have had a major impact on habitats around the world, building over natural landscapes and changing what grows there. Global warming is also having an effect on weather patterns and average temperatures, meaning that habitats are changing and animals now face different and more extreme challenges to survive.

Here is a look at some of the world's most interesting habitats and how they are beginning to change.

JUST DESERTS

A desert is an arid area where very little rain falls. Most receive less than 10 inches/254 millimeters of rain per year—around ten times less than a rainforest—which allows very little vegetation to grow.

BLOWING HOT AND COLD

Deserts can be divided into two varieties: hot deserts and cold deserts.

Cold deserts are iced over for some of the year, but the frozen water cannot be absorbed by plants.

Hot deserts can hit very high temperatures in the day, which causes the water to evaporate.

The Sahara Desert covers 3.5 million square miles/9 million square kilometers of the earth.

BORN SURVIVOR

Not many animals can live in these harsh conditions, but some creatures have adapted in amazing ways to survive.

DUNE ATTUNED

Dromedary camels make up 90 percent of the world's camel population.

They can drink up to 35 gallons of water in ten minutes!

Long eyelashes protect their eyes from blowing sands.

Wide feet stop them from sinking into the sand.

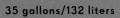
35 gallons/132 liters

SLEEP IT OFF

Many desert animals are nocturnal. They sleep under rocks and in underground burrows during the day to keep out of the hot temperatures.

Kangaroo rats and **scorpions** are both nocturnal.

GRASS IS GREENER

Grasslands are areas covered mostly with grasses. They are found on every continent except Antarctica.

WELL TEMPERED

Temperate grasslands can be found away from the coast. They have cold winters and warm, dry summers.

HOT TROPIC

Tropical grasslands are generally warm year-round and have a higher rainfall thanks to a wet season.

BIG OUTDOORS

Many of the world's large herbivores, such as bison, **giraffes, zebras,** and rhinoceroses, live in grasslands.

MOVING ON

Many of these animals form herds that migrate across the plains, following the rains and grazing on the grasses through the seasons.

THE CHASE IS ON

These herds are hunted by some of the world's biggest carnivores, such as **lions,** wolves, leopards, and cheetahs.

SMALL FORTUNE

Many smaller creatures thrive in the grasslands, including **butterflies,** beetles, mice, and moles.

59

POLES APART

The Arctic is situated at the North Pole, while the Antarctic can be found at the South Pole. Together they make up the polar regions — the world's coldest habitats.

STOP AND REFLECT

White Antarctic ice reflects more sun than it absorbs, which keeps Earth's temperature down.

ARCTIC

The Arctic is made up of islands of sea ice that drift around the North Pole.

It is iced over year-round, but the ice covered area expands in winter and shrinks in summer.

Polar bears have been known to travel up to 3,000 miles/ 4,828 kilometers in search of food.

BEAR NECESSITIES

Polar bears have adapted to live in the Arctic.

A thick, colorless coat reflects the sunlight and keeps them camouflaged and warm.

Large feet stop them from sinking into the snow and make them great swimmers.

BIG BIRD

Emperor penguins are the biggest — and the hardiest — of all the penguins. Large colonies group together in the Antarctic to breed.

An emperor penguin can dive up to 1,850 feet/564 meters, which is deeper than any bird!

ANTARCTIC

The Antarctic is land, but is also surrounded by ice — some of it over 1 mile/ 1.6 kilometers thick!

CHILLED OUT

Specially adapted to its environment, an **Arctic fox's** thick fur allows it to sleep in temperatures as cold as −50°F/−45.5°C without any problems.

Its paws are well supplied with blood, which prevents them from freezing in the snow.

TUNDRA

Around the poles is the tundra — a cold, treeless area where the ground stays frozen year-round.

Mosses, lichens, and shrubs can grow here and sustain **reindeer,** arctic hares, and lemmings, among other animals.

RAIN FOREST

Rain forests are home to half of all the living animal and plant species in the world. Up to 80 percent of all insects live there, with millions more thought to still be discovered!

UNDER THREAT

Rain forests are among the most threatened habitats in the world due to human deforestation.

WET AND WILD

Tropical rain forests are found near the equator and stay hot and humid all year. On average, they can receive up to 450 inches/1,143 centimeters of rain per year.

CANOPY

UNDERSTORY

FOREST FLOOR

MONKEYING ABOUT

Black spider monkeys use their tail as a fifth limb to grasp branches. They rarely come to the ground, feeding on fruit and nuts in the trees.

URBAN ARRAY

Urban habitats are areas where the natural landscape has been built over with human constructions.

Any animals that live here have to cope with unnatural sources of light, sound, and food. Some have adapted very successfully, including mice, pigeons, rats, squirrels and foxes.

GOING TO TOWN

Pigeons are a familiar sight in town squares around the world. They are the offspring of domestic pigeons that returned to the wild.

RATTED OUT

Rats like to live near humans, as food is often found nearby. They are considered pests because they steal food, damage property, and spread diseases.

CITY SLICKER

There is often a higher population of **foxes** in an urban environment compared to the surrounding countryside.

It's estimated that there are around 10,000 foxes living in London, England.

ROAD RAGE

60 percent of red foxes in Bristol, England, are killed by cars.

FARM FRIENDLY

Farmland—an area that has been cleared by humans to grow crops or rear animals for food—doesn't support the number of species that might live in the area naturally, but the fields are often bounded by hedgerows and forests where natural wildlife can be found.

BLOWN WIDE OPEN

Barn owls benefit from the wide open spaces found on farms. They are able to swoop down on mice and voles that are left exposed when they venture out in the flat fields.

HEDGED IN

Hedges are important for increasing the diversity of wildlife in an area. Records show that more than 600 plants, 1,500 insects, 65 birds, and 20 mammal species live or feed in hedgerows.

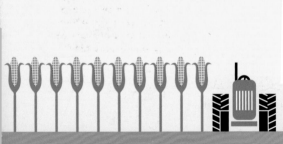

CROPPING UP

Fields of crops attract many kinds of insects, birds, and rodents, who feed on the plants. Some farmers use pesticides to kill the insects, so that less of their crop is destroyed.

HOT TOPIC

Habitats around the world are under threat because of global warming— a rise in the temperature of the earth's atmosphere. It is making deserts expand and get hotter, affecting weather patterns, reducing crop yields from farms, and melting ice in the polar regions.

COOKING WITH GAS

Global warming is caused by three gases in particular: carbon dioxide (CO_2), greenhouse gasses such as methane, and chlorofluorocarbons (CFCs).

WARMING UP

Some scientists predict that a baby born today will experience a global rise in temperature of 10.8°F/6.5°C in its lifetime.

MELT DOWN

Global warming means that ice in the polar regions is melting. Sea levels are rising because of this, leading to widespread flooding.

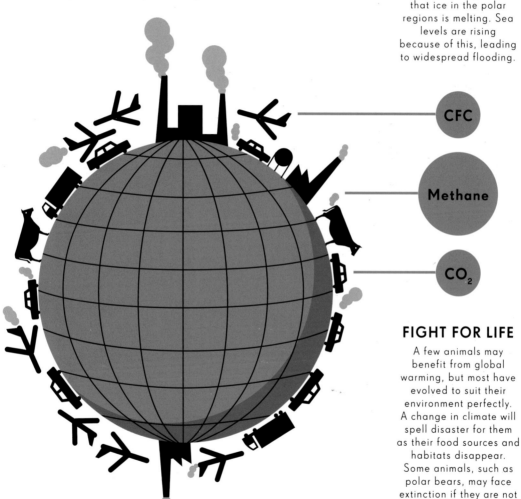

CFC

Methane

CO_2

FIGHT FOR LIFE

A few animals may benefit from global warming, but most have evolved to suit their environment perfectly. A change in climate will spell disaster for them as their food sources and habitats disappear. Some animals, such as polar bears, may face extinction if they are not properly protected.

GOOD ATMOSPHERE

The earth is warmed by rays of heat from the sun and is surrounded by an atmosphere that allows some of this heat to be reflected back out into space.

HOT HOUSE

Having too many greenhouse gases in the atmosphere stops heat from escaping, leading to a rise in the earth's temperature.

MAN-MADE

Greenhouse gases do occur naturally, but our reliance on fossil fuels and the destruction of the rain forests is speeding up the effects of global warming.

KILLERS

It's a dog-eat-dog world out in the wild, and many animals have to fight to survive.

Hunger is one of the main reasons that an animal will kill. Predators need to use deadly weapons — such as claws, teeth, and venom — to become successful hunters.

Their prey have had to develop some pretty tough defense mechanisms in response, and while they may not go looking for a fight, a tussle with some of these naturally docile creatures can have fatal consequences.

Some of nature's most savage battles can be fought between two animals of the same species. Fighting for mating rights ensures the strongest animal's genes will be passed on, and with such high stakes, these battles can be ferociously fought. Staking claim to the best patch of land can also be a matter of life or death to an animal, leading to fierce turf wars.

Take a look at some of the deadliest, strangest, and most underrated natural-born killers out there.

FIGHT CLUB

Many animals are forced to fight to ensure their survival. Here are some of the reasons why they turn to violence.

NO TRESPASSING

The area of land that an animal lives in is called its territory. This is where it finds food, rears its young, and keeps out of danger. It is so important to survival that many animals will kill for the rights to the best plot.

TURF WAR

Gangs of **monkeys** and **chimpanzees** will wage war on competing tribes to take over their territories.

The defending monkeys will scream and bark to scare off the attackers, rattling branches and throwing sticks and feces.

BIG BUCKS

Male **rabbits** are very territorial and will fight to the death to protect their land.

CROCODILE SHOO

Hippos will often attack — and sometimes kill — crocodiles for the best spot in the swamp.

KISS OF DEATH

In nature, females want to make sure that their offspring receive the strongest genes and are given the best chances of survival. This can make mating a dangerous business for the males, who sometimes have to fight to impress the females.

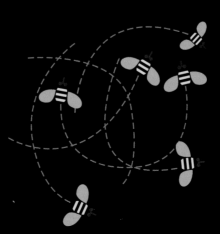

KILLER BEES

Male **Dawson's bees** engage in a fighting frenzy to be able to mate with females. The fighting leaves most of them (and many females) dead.

KILLER INSTINCT

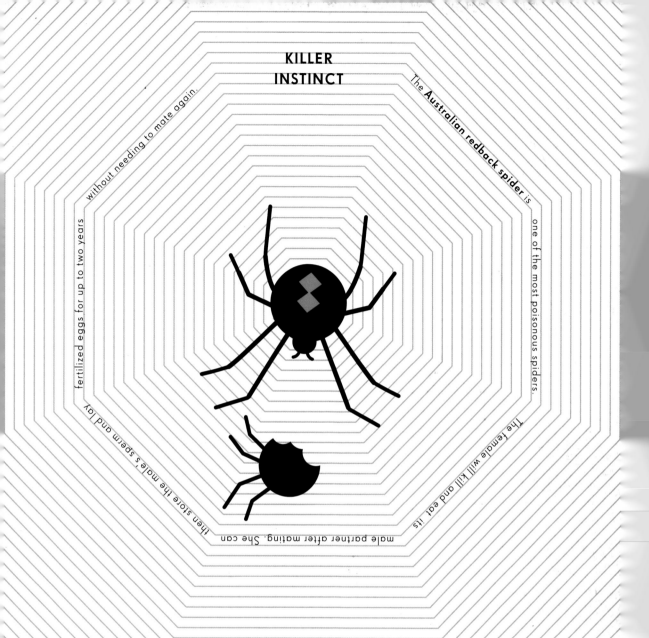

The **Australian redback spider** is one of the most poisonous spiders. The female will kill and eat its male partner after mating. She can then store the male's sperm and lay fertilized eggs for up to two years without needing to mate again.

DEADLY EMBRACE

Female **scorpions** often kill the males after they mate, injecting them with a series of lethal stings and eating them.

ROMANCE IS DEAD

In nature, some females have no more need for their partner once they have used them to mate, and simply kill them afterward.

Even in death, this can give the male an advantage over his rivals: once the female has eaten his body, she is unlikely to go looking for another mate, meaning his genes are the ones that will be passed on in the eggs the female lays.

KILLING MACHINE

Many animals are built to kill because they have to hunt for food to avoid starvation.

SILENT BUT DEADLY

Many animals are famed for their strength, speed, or deadly weaponry, but here are some of the most underrated predators.

NAUGHTY KITTY

Domestic **cats** kill between 1.4 and 3.7 billion birds and between 6.9 and 20.7 billion mammals a year in the United States.

LITTLE DEVIL

The **Tasmanian devil** is the world's largest marsupial. It has the strongest bite in comparison to its weight of any living mammal.

BADGER TO DEATH

The **honey badger** has sharp teeth, strong jaws, and long claws that it uses to kill and eat venomous snakes and to raid beehives for their honey. They can fight off much bigger animals—sometimes frightening away young lions to steal their food!

TONGUE LASHING

Chameleons have stereoscopic eyes and 360-degree vision, making it hard for prey to go undetected. With a tongue three times the length of its body, it can hit prey in thirty thousandths of a second.

69

SELF-DEFENSE

Many animals have developed bizarre — and sometimes deadly — ways to defend themselves from predators.

COOL AS A CUCUMBER

The **sea cucumber** can turn itself inside out, shooting its intestines out of its body to entangle predators.

SLIPPERY CHARACTER

The **hagfish** oozes a toxic slime when under attack, helping it to squirm out of danger.

KEPT ON ITS TOES

The **hairy frog** breaks the bones in its toes to produce "claws." The bones puncture the skin on its feet and are used as defensive weapons.

EYE-OPENER

The **horned lizard** can squirt foul-tasting blood from the corners of its eyes to scare off attackers. The jet of blood can travel up to 5 feet/1.5 meters.

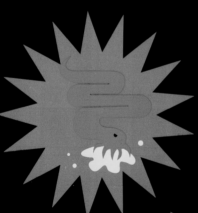

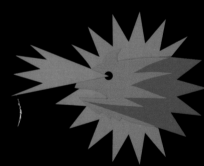

SHAKE, RATTLE, AND ROLL

The **crested porcupine** will rattle its tail quills as a threat, stabbing any attacker as a final resort — sometimes fatally

GETTING ANTSY

The **Malaysian soldier ant** has poison-filled glands inside its body. When it senses a threat, it explodes, spraying poison to protect its colony.

INSECTICIDE

The **bombardier beetle** sprays a mixture of boiling toxic chemicals from its abdomen that is fatal to other insects and makes a popping sound as it is released.

REEK OF DEATH

The **opossum** plays dead by slipping into a coma when it is attacked, foaming at the mouth and releasing a green liquid from its backside that smells like a corpse.

READY TO ROLL

The **pangolin** is covered in scales and rolls into a very tight ball — sometimes down a hill — to escape its enemies.

STICKY SITUATION

The **fulmar** launches a sticky orange goo at attackers. This substance glues other birds' feathers together so that they can't fly or swim.

HEADS OR TAILS

If a **dormouse** is caught by the tail, it can make its tail drop off, helping it to escape.

STAB IN THE BACK

The male **platypus** stabs enemies with its ankle spur, injecting them with a powerful poison.

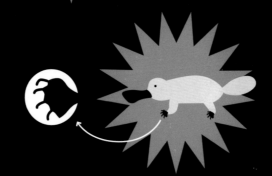

MAN'S BEST FRIEND

Ever since the last ice age, humans have lived and worked with dogs. Today's domesticated dogs evolved from wolves, which were used by early humans for hunting, protection, and pulling sleds. The special bond that was forged all those thousands of years ago has earned dogs the title of "man's best friend."

Because of their good temperament and high intelligence, dogs make excellent pets. However, with their agility, strength, and especially their excellent sense of smell, dogs can be useful even in today's technological world, coming to the rescue with their specialized abilities!

Over time, humans have bred many varieties of dogs. Some are prized for their good looks, and others are bred and trained to perform certain jobs, such as herding sheep, sniffing out trouble, or guiding the blind.

Read on to find out why dogs are still man's best friend.

WORK LIKE A DOG

Dogs aren't just great pets. Many breeds work for humans—sometimes even saving their lives.

TO THE RESCUE

Herding dogs make good mountain rescue animals and are accustomed to working with humans.

SNOWED UNDER

Humans lose around 40,000 scented skin cells per hour. Avalanche dogs are trained to sniff out these cells by burying their head in the snow. If the smell gets stronger, they keep digging. If it gets weaker, they start digging nearby until it's stronger again.

TOP DOG

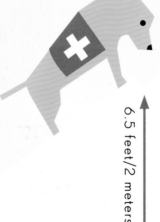

A team of twenty people searching for an avalanche victim expect to cover 2.5 acres/ 1 hectare of land in four hours. A mountain rescue dog can do it in thirty minutes—an eighth of the time.

DIG DEEP

Most dogs can find people buried under about 6.5 feet/2 meters of snow.

A man in the United States was found under 33 feet/10 meters of snow.

Another man, in Austria, was rescued beneath 39 feet/12 meters of snow.

6.5 feet/2 meters

WHIFF OF TROUBLE

German police collected scents from political activists to enable their dogs to trace people they believed might try to violently disrupt the 2007 G8 summit.

BERNARDS WORK HARD

The most famous Saint Bernard was named Barry. He was bred at the Great St. Bernard Hospice in Switzerland. He rescued forty people, most famously a young boy whom he discovered, maneuvered onto his back, and carried to safety.

Saint Bernards aren't often used as rescue dogs, and, contrary to legend, they never have small kegs of whiskey tied around their necks.

TIME MATTERS

Ninety percent of people buried in avalanches survive if they are recovered within fifteen minutes of being buried.

Only thirty percent survive after thirty minutes.

Just three percent live if buried for more than two hours.

DEATH SCENT

When emergency services are searching for a body rather than a living person they need a different kind of dog: a cadaver dog, trained to detect rotting flesh.

SEEING DOGS

Guide dogs help visually impaired and blind people by safely navigating them about.

SMELL A RAT

Dogs are used to sniff other things too, such as . . .

cash   explosives   drugs

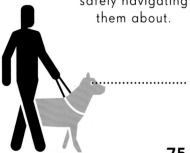

DOG BONES

Dogs come in all shapes and sizes,
but they share the same body parts.

BRAIN

Dogs' brains have evolved to become
smaller since humans domesticated them.
A four-month-old wolf pup in the wild has
a bigger brain than a fully grown dog.

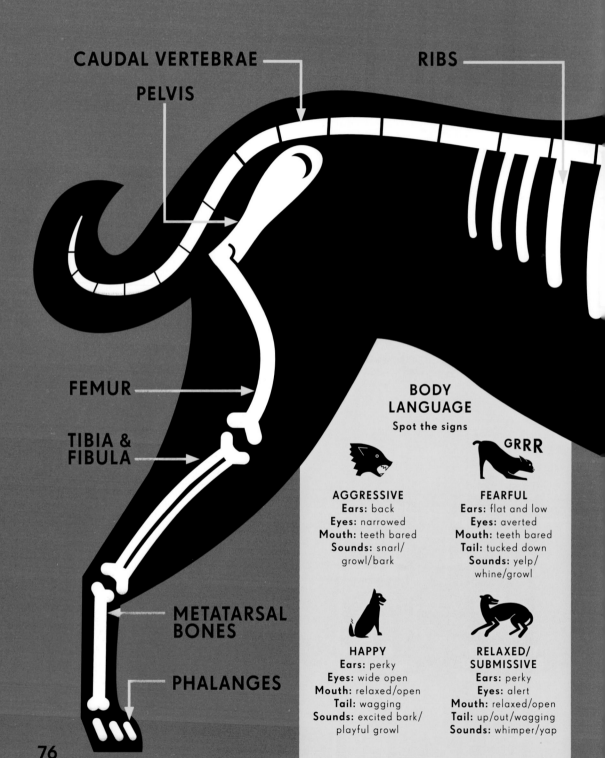

CAUDAL VERTEBRAE

PELVIS

RIBS

FEMUR

TIBIA &
FIBULA

METATARSAL
BONES

PHALANGES

BODY LANGUAGE
Spot the signs

AGGRESSIVE
Ears: back
Eyes: narrowed
Mouth: teeth bared
Sounds: snarl/
growl/bark

GRRR

FEARFUL
Ears: flat and low
Eyes: averted
Mouth: teeth bared
Tail: tucked down
Sounds: yelp/
whine/growl

HAPPY
Ears: perky
Eyes: wide open
Mouth: relaxed/open
Tail: wagging
Sounds: excited bark/
playful growl

**RELAXED/
SUBMISSIVE**
Ears: perky
Eyes: alert
Mouth: relaxed/open
Tail: up/out/wagging
Sounds: whimper/yap

NASAL CAVITY

ESOPHAGUS

TRACHEA

SCAPULA

HAPPY WAGGING
Usually, dogs wag their tails to express happiness. However . . .

when dogs feel positive about someone, their tails wag more to the right . . .

and when they have negative feelings, their tail wagging is biased to the left.

LUNGS

HEART

HUMERUS

RADIUS & ULNA

METACARPAL BONES

PHALANGES

BEST IN SHOW

Many dogs were originally bred to work for humans—although they are often more likely to be pets now. See what they were designed for in the first place.

COLLIE
Herding livestock and working.

JACK RUSSELL
Accompanying fox hunts.

DOBERMAN PINSCHER
Protecting humans—often used as guard and police dogs.

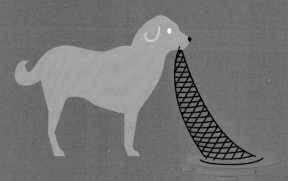

LABRADOR RETRIEVER
Helping fishermen retrieve their catch by pulling nets in from the water.

BOXER
Chasing down and holding prey.

KUVASZ
Owned and bred only by aristocracy for hunting and guarding.

WOOF!

TERRIER
Catching rats, rabbits, and foxes.

BLACK RUSSIAN TERRIER
Guard dogs
for the Soviet army.

CHIHUAHUA
Bred as a pet in
ancient Mexico.

ANATOLIAN SHEPHERD
Guarding sheep and goats.

GREAT DANE
Guarding — bred in
ancient Egypt for ferocity.

STANDARD POODLE
Hunting and retrieving waterfowl.

SAMOYED
Pulling sleds.

First U.S. edition 2014

Library of Congress Catalog Card Number 2013944025
ISBN 978-0-7636-7122-8

13 14 15 16 17 18 CCP 10 9 8 7 6 5 4 3 2 1

Printed in Shenzhen, Guangdong, China

This book was typeset in Super Grotesk.
The illustrations were created digitally.

BIG PICTURE PRESS
an imprint of
Candlewick Press
99 Dover Street
Somerville, Massachusetts 02144

www.candlewick.com
www.bigpicturepress.net